TRADITIONS AND CELEBRATIONS

RAMADAN AND EID AL-FITR

by Melissa Ferguson

PEBBLE
a capstone imprint

Pebble Explore is published by Pebble, an imprint of Capstone.
1710 Roe Crest Drive
North Mankato, Minnesota 56003
www.capstonepub.com

Library of Congress Cataloging-in-Publication Data
Names: Ferguson, Melissa, author.
Title: Ramadan and Eid al-Fitr / by Melissa Ferguson.
Description: North Mankato, Minnesota : Pebble, 2021. | Series: Pebble Explore. Traditions & celebrations | Includes bibliographical references and index. | Audience: Ages 6-8 | Audience: Grades 2-3 |
Summary: "Ramadan is an Islamic holy month. During this holiday, some Muslims fast from sunrise to sunset, read from the Quran, or pray. Others help the poor, hang lanterns, or make crafts and decorations. Readers will discover how a shared holiday can have multiple traditions and be celebrated in all sorts of ways"-- Provided by publisher.
Identifiers: LCCN 2020038013 (print) | LCCN 2020038014 (ebook) | ISBN 9781977131904 (hardcover) | ISBN 9781977132925 (paperback) | ISBN 9781977154781 (pdf) | ISBN 9781977156440 (kindle edition) Subjects: LCSH: Ramadan--Juvenile literature. | ʿĪd al-Fiṭr--Juvenile literature.
Classification: LCC BP186.4 .F47 2021 (print) | LCC BP186.4 (ebook) | DDC 297.3/62--dc23 LC record available at https://lccn.loc.gov/2020038013 LC ebook record available at https://lccn.loc.gov/2020038014

Image Credits
iStockphoto/SolStock, 26, 27; Shutterstock: arapix, 28, dotshock, 12, Feroze Edassery, cover, 1, 11, Fevziie, 29, FS Stock, 17, Herlanzer, 8, JOAT, 6, kamomeen, 14, Kertu, 18, leolintang, 15, Maya Afzaal, 20, Odua Images, 24, Orhan Cam, 25, Pixel-Shot, 16, Rido, 22, Yusnizam Yusof, 5, ZouZou, 9, Zurijeta, 13, 19, 21

Artistic elements: Shutterstock/Rafal Kulik

Editorial Credits
Designer: Sarah Bennett; Media Researcher: Kelly Garvin; Production Specialist: Spencer Rosio

Consultant
Nahid Khan

All internet sites appearing in back matter were available and accurate when this book was sent to press.

TABLE OF CONTENTS

WHAT IS RAMADAN? 4

WHEN IS RAMADAN? 6

WHAT DOES FASTING MEAN? 8

SUHOOR 10

IFTAR 12

THE QUR'AN AND PRAYER..................... 14

ACTS OF KINDNESS................................. 18

RAMADAN AT SCHOOL 22

EID AL-FITR 24

GLOSSARY 30

READ MORE.................................... 31

INTERNET SITES 31

INDEX... 32

HOW TO SAY IT 32

Words in **bold** are in the glossary.

WHAT IS RAMADAN?

It is a quiet night at home. Ayesha is with her family. They are reading from the Qur'an. It is the holy book of Islam. People who follow the **religion** of Islam are called Muslims.

It is the start of the month of Ramadan. This Muslim holiday is **celebrated** around the world. During Ramadan, Muslims pray to God. They **fast** during the day. They spend time with loved ones. They try to become better people.

WHEN IS RAMADAN?

Muslims use a **lunar calendar**. Ramadan is the ninth month of the lunar calendar. It begins when the first **crescent moon** is seen after sunset.

The lunar calendar is a little shorter than the **solar calendar**. Each solar year, Ramadan happens about 11 days sooner than the year before. As years pass, Ramadan comes in different seasons.

Muslim children watch for the crescent moon in the sky. It is exciting to begin the month of Ramadan!

WHAT DOES FASTING MEAN?

One important part of Ramadan is fasting. Fasting is choosing to not eat or drink for a reason. Many Muslims fast from **dawn** until sunset during Ramadan.

Fasting helps Muslims learn to be patient. It reminds them to be grateful. It also reminds them to help people who are in need.

Not everyone is able to fast during Ramadan. Small children do not need to fast. Sick or elderly people may also choose not to fast.

SUHOOR

During Ramadan, Muslim families rise very early. They eat a Suhoor meal together before dawn.

Healthy foods are served. Suhoor might include **lentils**, beans, eggs, fruits, juices, and water. These help people feel less hungry and thirsty during the day.

The Suhoor meal ends with a **prayer** at dawn. It is the first prayer of the day.

IFTAR

After sunset, Muslims end their fast. They eat a light Iftar meal. It begins with dried fruit called dates. Iftar gives energy to the body.

The Iftar meal begins with dates.

After Iftar is a prayer. It is the sunset prayer. Then a larger meal is served. It may have soup, fish, chicken, or other meat. Vegetables, rice, bread, and dessert are also served. People come together for a delicious meal!

THE QUR'AN AND PRAYER

Ramadan is a special month. Muslims celebrate that God began to teach the Qur'an to the **Prophet Muhammad**. Muslims believe this happened more than 1,400 years ago during Ramadan.

Qur'an

Reading the Qur'an is a part of Muslims' **worship**. Many Muslims read a part each day during Ramadan. Ramadan lasts 29 or 30 days. Some people read the whole Qur'an during the month.

Muslims pray five times each day. The first prayer is at dawn. There are also prayers at noon, mid-afternoon, and sunset. The last prayer is at night.

Praying at a mosque

A mother shows her son prayer beads.

Prayer is especially important during the month of Ramadan. **Mosques** hold a large worship service each night of Ramadan.

Muslims may pray at a mosque or pray at home. As children get older, they learn to pray with their parents.

ACTS OF KINDNESS

Ramadan is also a time for acts of kindness. It is a time for Muslims of all ages to work on good behavior. Mosques hold large dinners to feed people in need. They raise money to help others.

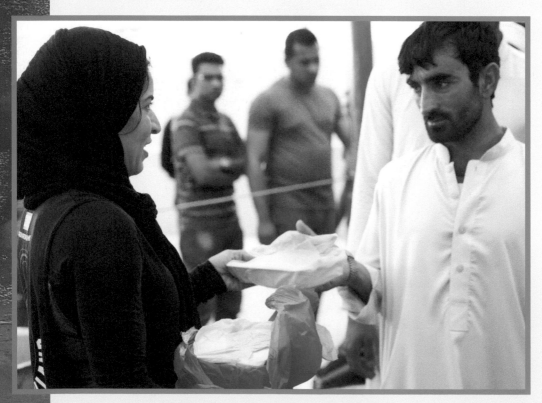

Families might buy toys for a **shelter**. They might help an older neighbor. They might make a basket of food for someone in need. They offer help to people who need it.

Muslim children do not need a lot of money to help others. During Ramadan, they may make a card for a relative. They might set the table for dinner. Saying something nice about someone is a kind act. Even a smile can make another person happy.

If you are not Muslim, you can still help celebrate the holiday. You could join Muslim friends in doing acts of kindness.

RAMADAN AT SCHOOL

Many students learn about religions at school. This helps them understand how people live in their neighborhood and around the world.

Here are some ways students can learn about Ramadan at school:

- Read books about Ramadan and Muslim children.

- Watch a video about how Muslim families celebrate Ramadan.

- Ask a Muslim teacher or parent to visit your school.

- Make a Ramadan dessert!

Learn to say "Ramadan Mubarak" to Muslim friends and neighbors. This means "Blessed Ramadan."

EID AL-FITR

Ramadan ends with the first crescent moon of the next month. Then three days of celebration begin! It is called Eid al-Fitr. It means "Festival of Breaking the Fast."

Islamic Center and Mosque of Washington, D.C.

During Eid al-Fitr, many Muslims come together to pray. There are large services at mosques or in open spaces. They listen to a sermon. People may come from far away. Muslims say "Eid Mubarak!" This greeting means "Blessed Festival!"

Eid al-Fitr is a happy time. Muslims
visit family and friends. They welcome
guests to their homes. They clean
and decorate. New clothes are worn.
Delicious meals and sweets are served.
Children are given gifts or candy.

Families also give food and money to help people in need. They send cards to loved ones. They forgive people who have made them unhappy. They spend time with family and friends. They enjoy feasts!

Remember Ayesha and her family? They are celebrating Eid al-Fitr! Ayesha and her father made cookies. They will share them with guests. Ayesha helped get the house ready for an Eid party.

Soon the Eid guests will arrive. Relatives and friends will celebrate together. It is a happy time for Muslims all around the world.

GLOSSARY

celebrate (SELL-uh-brayt)—to do something special for an event or holiday

crescent moon (KRESS-uhnt MOON)—an early stage of the moon when less than half can be seen; it is shaped like a C

dawn (DAHN)—the first light of morning

fast (FAST)—to give up food or drink for a period of time for a reason

lentil (LEN-tuhl)—a seed related to beans and peas

lunar calendar (LOON-uhr CAL-uhn-duhr)—a calendar based on the cycles of the moon

mosque (MOHSK)—a place of prayer for Muslims

prayer (PREHR)—words or thoughts sent to a god

Prophet Muhammad (PRAH-fuht muh-HAHM-ed)—the person Muslims believe was the last in a series of prophets who taught about God; he lived about 1,400 years ago in western Arabia

religion (reh-LIH-juhn)—the belief in a god or gods

shelter (SHEL-tuhr)—a place that provides food and a bed to people without homes

solar calendar (SOH-lurh CAL-uhn-duhr)—a calendar based on the position of Earth as it moves around the sun

worship (WOHR-ship)—religious practice

READ MORE

Khan, Ausma Zehanat. *Ramadan: The Holy Month of Fasting.* Custer, WA: Orca Book Publishers, 2018.

Lumbard, Rabiah York. *The Gift of Ramadan.* Chicago: Albert Whitman & Company, 2019.

Sebra, Richard. *It's Ramadan and Eid Al-Fitr!* Minneapolis: Lerner Publications, 2017.

INTERNET SITES

Celebrating Ramadan
kids.nationalgeographic.com/explore/history/ramadan/

Ramadan
pbslearningmedia.org/resource/c242a960-8ebc-43c3-a155-b985b78a719d/ramadan/#.XpDw4jrYq3A

Ramadan & Eid ul-Fitr
pbskids.org/arthur/holidays/ramadan-and-eid-ul-fitr/

INDEX

children, 7, 9, 17, 20

crescent moon, 6–7, 24

dawn, 8, 10–11, 16

fasting, 4, 8–9, 12

foods, 10, 12–13, 26, 28

forgiveness, 27

gifts, 26

helpfulness, 9, 19, 27

Iftar, 12–13

kindness, 18–21

length of Ramadan, 14

lunar calendar, 6–7

mosques, 17, 18, 25

prayer, 4, 11, 13, 16–17, 25

Prophet Muhammad, 14

Qur'an, 4, 14

solar calendar, 7

Suhoor, 10–11

sunset, 6, 8, 12–13, 16

HOW TO SAY IT

Eid al-Fitr
(eed al-fitter)

Eid Mubarak
(eed mu-bahr-ak)

Iftar
(IFF-tahr)

Islam
(ISS-lahm)

Muslim
(MUSS-lim)

Qur'an
(kur-AHN)

Ramadan
(rah-muh-DAHN)

Suhoor
(sa-HOOR)